Ledgard of
Buses

A celebration of Sammy's blue buses

STUART EMMETT

KEY
Books

BRITAIN'S BUSES SERIES, VOLUME 1

Cover image: Ex-Ribble BCK422 is passing the main entrance to Leeds University, just out of sight to the right of the bus. (Tony Greaves)

Title page image: 1954U passes the West Yorkshire coach station on Wellington Street, Leeds. (Tony Greaves)

Contents page image: LAE2 at Chester Street bus station, Bradford. (John L May)

Published by Key Books
An imprint of Key Publishing Ltd
PO Box 100
Stamford
Lincs
PE19 1XQ

www.keypublishing.com

The right of Stuart Emmett to be identified as the author of this book has been asserted in accordance with the Copyright, Designs and Patents Act 1988 Sections 77 and 78.

Copyright © Stuart Emmett, 2020

ISBN 978 1 913295 85 1

20 21 22 23 24   10 9 8 7 6 5 4 3 2 1

Typeset by Aura Technology and Software Services, India.

Contents

Introduction

This is not a definitive history of Ledgard, as others have already done this (Bate and Jenkinson for example, see References). This book is, however, pure nostalgia using pictures, with illustrative captions, to rekindle memories for those fortunate enough to have known Ledgard's buses and, also, to give an insight to the many others who were never able to experience them first-hand.

The book starts with a brief look at the history of Ledgard and then at the routes operated, after which the fleet will be examined. This is done by centring on the ex-London HGF's Daimlers that ran on all but two of the double-decker routes. Next are the single-decker buses and the low-bridge double deckers that operated the two Otley to Horsforth routes.

These two central themes are then related and connected to all the other Ledgard buses in the post-war fleet and continue until the sale of Ledgard to West Yorkshire in 1967, when we lost Ledgard, an operator of special interest and undoubted charm.

Unless stated below, the pictures are from my own collection, which is made up of our family pictures and ones from other sources. For the latter, where the original photographer cannot be traced, I offer my apologies to them for the lack of accreditation and would be pleased to correct this in any future edition.

Pictures/images are from the following people, in no specific order. I am so grateful to them all for their work, foresight and diligence over the years; especially also for sharing their work and not keeping images locked away.

- J S Cockshott, care of Michael Eyre from Robin Fell at the Transport Library.
- Geoff Lumb, from Tony Wilson at Travel Lens Photographic (TLP). TLP also provided many other images.
- Phil Moth at P M Photography.
- Tony Greaves from the Samuel Ledgard Society.
- Chris Howard at Bus Photos UK.
- Neil Halliday from the Escrick Bus & Coach Archive.
- David Beilby from the GEC Collection.
- Roy Marshall, care of Alan Oxley at the Omnibus Society (OS).
- Chris Ashton at Omnicolour.
- John L May and Harry Luff, care of Peter Waller at the Online Transport Archive (OTA).

Proceeds from the sale of this book will, after expenses, be passed on to those who continue to uphold the memory of Ledgard.

Chapter 1

History

S amuel Ledgard, the legendary founder and owner of the bus operator based in Leeds, started out in business by taking on his father's pub, the Nelson Hotel in Armley, in 1896. Soon Sammy (as he was colloquially known) branched out into outside catering at race meetings and agricultural shows by providing tents, catering equipment, staff, food and drink. For this transport was needed and so a lorry, registered U 1949, was purchased in 1912. Forty-five years on, this registration would be used in reverse form when six new AEC Regent Vs with local Roe bodies were bought and registered 1949 U to 1954 U.

The original U 1949 acquired an interchangeable coach body, and services to the seaside resorts of Scarborough and Blackpool started in 1913, when two further convertible vehicles were acquired. The 1914 to 1918 war stopped any expansion, but in 1920, four coaches along with four convertible ones resumed the coastal runs.

From 1920 onwards, Ledgard purchased many local bus operators, along with their vehicles; the main route network was built in 20 years. The main fleet was always bought new, with Leylands being the preferred choice. However, the death of Samuel Ledgard in April 1952 gave birth to a new era when the Executors of Samuel Ledgard, led by his son Tom, changed policy towards buying second-hand buses.

In the next 15 years, only 13 new vehicles were obtained but over 170 second-hand ones joined the fleet. Additionally, the two subsidiary companies, Cream Bus Service Limited (founded in 1924) and the 1928 B and B Tours, became S Ledgard (Ilkley) and S Ledgard (Bradford) Limited respectively; the latter, at times, had used the Bradford AK/KW/KY registrations for their new vehicles.

Ledgard often bought interesting and different buses like DCN838 from Northern General in Gateshead, which was one of eight they put in service in 1963. (TLP)

Chapter 2

Routes

Route details from the 1950s follow from the referenced timetable date. The timetable was a stapled collection of duplicated individual sheets per route, the sheets having many different typewriter fonts (it could be described as 'rustic').

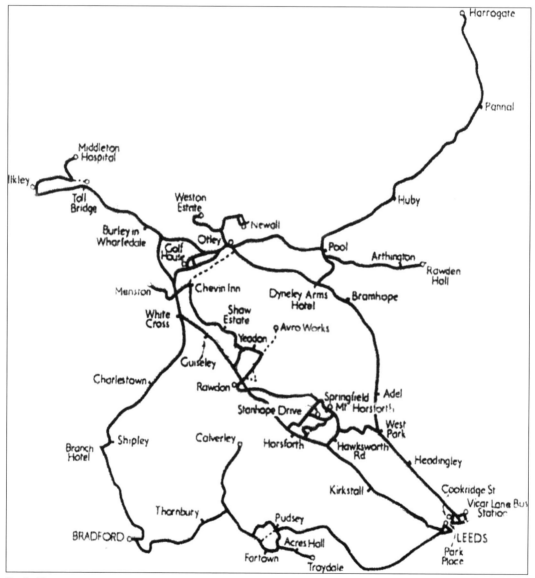

Route Map

Route List

Route	Journey time in Minutes	Maximum headway in Minutes	Maximum number of buses required (excluding duplicates)	Depot allocation	Timetable date and comments plus start date of route
Leeds (King St*), Guiseley to Ilkley	53	30	4	1 bus from Armley and 3 buses from Otley & Ilkley	April 1953. Started 1927.
Leeds (Cookridge St), Bramhope, Otley to Ilkley	34 to Otley, plus 21 to Ilkley	20 to Otley 60 to Ilkley	3 2	Armley Otley & Ilkley	October 1958 and a joint route with West Yorkshire RCC who had 27.6% of the mileage. Started 1924 to Otley and 1925 to Ilkley.
Leeds (King St*), Pudsey, Fartown to Bradford	47	15	8	Armley & Bradford	June 1958. Started 1924 to Pudsey and 1926 to Bradford.
Leeds (King St*), Kirkstall, Hawksworth Road to Horsforth	25	30	2	Armley	December 1958. Hawkesworth Road was a common spelling mistake on the bus blinds. Started 1924.
Leeds (Vicar Lane), Headingley, West Park, Horsforth to Rawdon	35	30	3	Armley	June 1958 and a joint route with West Yorkshire (not on Sundays). Started 1943.
Troydale, or Acres Hall (both in Pudsey) to Calverley	27	30	2	1 from Armley (Troydale) 1 from Bradford (Acres Hall)	June 1958. Routes bought from Kitchin & Sons in April 1957.
Bradford, Menston, Otley to Harrogate	75	60	3	Bradford	June 1958. Started 1935.

Route	Journey time in Minutes	Maximum headway in Minutes	Maximum number of buses required (excluding duplicates)	Depot allocation	Timetable date and comments plus start date of route
Otley to Weston	10	30	1	Otley	March 1959. Started 1953.
Newall, Otley to Westbourne	10	30	1	Otley	No date shown. Started 1936 and 1949.
Otley to Arthington, some via Dyneley Arms from June 1964	15	2 journeys a day Mon–Sat (with 3 on Fridays)		Otley	June 1958. Started 1955 (formerly a 1934 route to Wetherby).
Ilkley to Middleton Sanatorium	12	3 journeys a week (Wed/ Sat/Sun)		Otley with Ilkley staff	June 1958. Started 1942.
Otley to Horsforth via West Chevin	55/60	60	2	Moorfield depot at Yeadon	December 1958. Started 1934.
Otley to Horsforth via White Cross	50/55	60	2	Moorfield Yeadon	June 1958. Started 1934.

* In 1964, due to a new one-way scheme on King Street, it changed to nearby Park Place.

In 1957, Ledgard's top-earning routes per mile were as follows:

   1st – Otley–Horsforth.
   2nd – Leeds–Guiseley–Ilkley.
   3rd – Leeds–Hawksworth Road–Horsforth.
   4th – Leeds–Bradford.

All routes were double-decker operated, although initially, the two Otley to Horsforth routes used single deckers. However, in early 1959, low-bridge double deckers replaced them.

   Bradford had restrictions on Ledgard's buses. Like the red West Yorkshire buses, they were prevented from loading in the lower town centre to protect Bradford CT.

   Ledgard's Leeds route, when inbound to Bradford, came from Thornbury roundabout, to the bottom area of Leeds Road, and then turned left up Vicar Lane, before going right at the top onto Croft Street and then over the railway and across Nelson Street to Manchester Road. Here the buses turned right, ran past the Odeon cinema and then left up Little Horton Lane for Chester Street bus station. Effectively, this took them round three sides of a square!

Outbound they went across Morley Street, right onto Great Horton Road (from where Ledgard moved their Bradford to Leeds terminus to Chester Street BS in 1947), and then past the Alhambra theatre to Town Hall Square and up to the Nelson Street traffic lights. Here came a left turn onto Croft Street, before taking the next left onto Vicar Lane for a right turn onto Leeds Road for Thornbury roundabout. However, from June 1964, due to redevelopment, the route outbound to Leeds stopped going to Town Hall Square and Nelson Street to Croft Street, and now left the same way as the inbound buses, using Manchester Road to get to Croft Street and onto Leeds Road.

Meanwhile, the Harrogate route in Bradford followed the West Yorkshire buses from Chester Street bus station to John Street for Manningham Lane and thereafter went through the upper part of the town centre.

On 26 Janaury 1957, JUM377 is leaving Bradford, still in 1946 livery, with the Town Hall behind, heading out of Town Hall Square for Nelson Street. In the middle backgound is the start and bottom of Leeds Road, which JUM377 will join further out of the city centre. Two of Bradford CT's AEC Regent/Weymann in the FKY1 to 40 batch can be seen on the Great Horton Road routes. (JS Cockshott)

HGF888 storms into Bradford on John Street from Harrogate. (TLP)

Depots

Allocations to the depots, including coaches, were as follows:

- Armley (in Leeds) with around 60 buses.
- Otley with around 20 vehicles.
- Bradford with around 10 vehicles.
- Ilkley was a running depot to Otley and had no permanent allocation and around four buses 'slept over' there.
- Moorfield in Yeadon (originally in the Rawdon parish area) with around ten.

Chapter 3

Fleet

Any historical presentation of Ledgard buses shows the many livery variations, especially throughout the 1950s. The following gives the main changes. However, as is well noted on the Old Buses website, 'countless combinations of dark and light blue, black, green and white were tried'. Therefore, the list below is not definitive.

Livery by Year	Below lower windows	Lower band (below lower windows)	Lower window frame surround	Mid band (waistband) above lower windows	Upper area below upper windows	Upper band below upper windows	Upper window frame surround	Roof
1930	Light blue	Dark blue	White	White	Light blue	Dark blue	White	Green
1946	Mid-blue	Dark blue	White	White	Mid-blue	Dark blue	White	Green
1952	Mid-blue	Mid-blue	White	White	Mid-blue	Mid-blue	Mid-blue	Green
1953	Mid-blue, some were dark blue	Light blue, with dark blue lining	Mid-blue	Light blue, in 1954 some got a white waistband	Mid-blue	Light blue, with dark blue lining	Mid-blue	Mid-blue
1955	Dark blue	Dark blue	Dark blue	White	Dark blue	White	Dark blue	Green
1959	Medium blue	Medium blue	Light grey	Light grey	Medium blue	Medium blue	Light grey	Light grey

Notes

- Light blue was also reported as pale blue or sky blue; dark blue as royal blue; mid- or medium blue as Nile blue, and light grey as battleship grey or duck-egg blue.
- The green roof was said to reflect the original fabric on the charabanc buses that were treated with green colour dope.
- The 1952 livery was first used on the PNWs that were new in 1952.
- The 1953 three-blue livery was first seen in April on HGF897 and 913 followed by a trial on HUA848 in May; HUA848 was withdrawn five months later.
- The 1959 livery was inspired by the two single deckers purchased from Baxters of Airdrie; the single deckers EWO/FAX introduced it, and PNW92 was the first double decker to have it.
- Coaches from 1959 to 1964 were Nile blue and buttery cream with a black roof; then, after 1964 they followed the dealer's stock coaches livery with light blue and cream livery.
- Single deckers at Moorfield, when initially re-allocated from coach to stage work, had the cream downward stripe painted light or sky blue,

As mentioned earlier, the initial vehicle choice was to buy new Leylands with the double deckers being all Leylands and single deckers being used on the Otley to Horsforth routes; these will be examined later.

11

Taking 1939 as a starting point, in that year HUA846 to 849 and four TD5s were acquired. In 1940, three more registered, JNW288 to 290. All these had Leyland H56R bodies and were ordered before the start of the 1939 to 1945 hostilities. The HUAs were withdrawn in 1953/54 and the JNWs in respectively 1955, 1957 and 1958.

HUA846 crosses the River Wharfe bridge in Otley, bound for Newall. In 1957, a concrete cantilevered foot walk was added on the left and the road then became two-way.

JNW289 from 1940 is in one of the 1953 experimental liveries and is pictured on Abbey Road, Kirkstall, inbound to Leeds. It was withdrawn in 1957.

The Second World War, when utility vehicles and 'you got what you could' ruled, saw the arrival of five Bedford OWBs, two Guy Arabs and 14 Daimlers CWs. Whilst the single-decked OWBs will be looked at in the later Moorfield route section (see page 51), we look here at the others.

From 1943 came JUA762 and 763 with Pickering utility bodies which were rebodied by Roe in 1951. In 1956, they received larger Gardner 6LW engines with an elongated radiator. They were withdrawn in 1961.

JUA762 is at the outskirts of Pudsey, on the route from Leeds to Bradford, with its 1951 Roe body. (Geoff Lumb)

In 1944 came JUA915 to 918, Daimler CWA6 type chassis with Roe UH56R bodies. They had varied lengths of service before being withdrawn in 1955, 1961, 1954 and 1959 respectively. Before then they were rebuilt by Ledgard with standard indicators.

JUA916 on a misty day on Cookridge Street, Leeds, was the last of the batch to be withdrawn. (P M Photography)

In 1945 came a batch of ten buses, registered JUB128/129, 647 to 652 and 658/659. All were CWA6s (apart from 647/648 that were CWD6s) with Duple bodies. They were withdrawn between 1953 and 1962.

This wonderful picture of 1945 JUB128 with a Duple body shows the bus climbing up Woodhall Road, Calverley. It will soon be at the top of the hill with views on the right side across to Eccleshill in Bradford and beyond to Ilkley Moor, and on the left side, down into Leeds. Hidden in the valley behind JUB128 is the River Aire, and on the horizon to the left is Guiseley and to the right is Yeadon. JUB128 was withdrawn in 1959. (P M Photography)

1945 JUB650 leaves Chester Street, Bradford, in a 1953 livery.

JUB648 in the 1959 livery is having a wheel changed in the entrance to Otley depot. It was the last of the JUB buses to be withdrawn in December 1962. (TLP)

JUB649 is not what it seems. On examination in 1953 it was condemned in a Certificate of Fitness inspection, due to bodywork corrosion on its overhauled chassis. As delivery was underway on the ex-London HGFs, the body from HGF948 was transferred to JUB649, whilst the chassis of HGF948 got the body from CUB1. In the 1955 livery, JUB649 is passing the Woodman Inn in Headingley, inbound to Leeds from Ilkley.

Ex-London CWA6 HGF948 was rebodied as FC31F using the 1935 Brush body from Ledgard's 1935 Maudslay SF40 coach registered CUB1 (seen later in original condition).

As we will soon see, these 14 utility Daimlers had a profound effect on Ledgard's purchases in the 1950s. However, immediately after the war ended, the pre-war buying policy continued and from 1946 until 1952, Ledgard bought 12 all Leyland PD1/PD2s.

In 1946 came six all Leyland PD1s, JUM373 to 378. They were withdrawn between October 1962 and January 1965.

1946 Leyland PD1 JUM373 is pictured outside Otley depot. JUM373 had a Leyland subcontracted Lancashire Aviation body and looks to be in the 1946 livery but without the white window frames.

JUM375 in Chester Street, Bradford, with the 1946 green-roofed livery and dark blue bands with white windows. (C Carter/Online Transport Archive)

JUM376 in the 1959 livery at Otley bus station. (Tony Greaves)

Three all Leylands came in 1949, registered MUA860 to 862. All were withdrawn in 1966.
   MUA862 is at Bradford in the 1946 livery but with a darker not mid-blue. It does still have dark blue bands below white windows and a green roof.

MUA862 in the 1955 livery is leaving Aire Street, Leeds, from City Square and is at the junction with Thirsk Row. It is entering Whitehall Road, which it followed for a few miles to Wortley Ringways roundabout before turning towards Pudsey and Fartown.

An MUA for Bradford on Infirmary Street, Leeds, is passing a Leeds CT on the 29 to Middleton and a Bradford CT Regent V on the direct route 72 that was joint with Leeds. Ledgard took 47 minutes to get to Bradford, and the direct 72 took 35 minutes.

MUA861 got new rounded windows after being rebuilt in January 1960 by Maudslay of Leeds following an accident; it also gained silver-sided strips to the engine cover. MUA861 is on Little Horton Lane amid Bradford centre's redevelopment and is a short distance from Chester Street bus station. (Tony Greaves)

In early 1952 came three Leyland PD2/12s with Leyland H56R bodies registered PNW91 to 93 that stayed until 1967. PNW91 is parked at Otley bus station in the 1952 livery that had no dark blue bands. Alongside, is an ex-London HGF delivered between 1953 and 1955. (TLP)

PNW92 waits to come on stand at Chester Street for Harrogate and was the first double decker in service with the 1959 livery. The car is parked on Chester Street, which was used for express buses. The Ledgard RT is loading for Leeds on the north side, which was also used by Hebble, Yorkshire Woollen, Yorkshire Traction and Sheffield JOC. (TLP)

The above has largely described the double-decker fleet up to the major changes for Ledgard brought about by the death of Mr Samuel Ledgard in April 1952. With his almost dictatorship rule of the company, lack of management delegation and the absence of records, the company was left in a poor state. His will made no mention of the future of the transport business, but his son, Tom, announced that his father's last wishes were given to him verbally and the bus business was to continue.

Therefore, the new management set about cleaning up the business, starting by selling for scrap the remains of 43 old vehicles that were in store and also 'modernising' the recent eight new half-cab Leyland PS/Duple coaches with full fronts (as shown later on pages 83 and 84). The payment of death duties did not help the company's financial liquidity, and the need to replace the pre-war Leyland double deckers was now paramount.

A second-hand source of buses was found locally at the local Leeds dealers, Norths, who had a quantity of London Transport Daimler CWA6s with mainly Park Royal H56R bodies. These had been new in 1946 with relaxed utility bodies that had rounded domes and moquette seats but still had single-skinned bodies with external roof framing. They were bought by London because, like most operators in the post-war period, they had an immediate need for vehicles and it would be some time before their new RTs would enter service. In the meantime, London's mixed fleet of buses was well past their sell-by date, and many of them had also been built to wartime utility standards. London had 756 utilities coming from chassis builders Bristol (29), Daimler (281), Guy (435) and Leyland (11) with bodies by Duple, Massey, Park Royal and Northern Coachbuilders.

The history of the London Daimler Park Royals started in 1946, when London Transport accepted an allocation from the Ministry of Supply of 100 Daimlers and London insisted they had CWA6 chassis with AEC engines. They then looked for a body builder, and with the promise of huge volume from the future RTs, they approached Park Royal and Weymann. Weymann, however, could not help but Park Royal did, providing London did not have the post-war metal-framed body, but only got those of composite construction. These used the available unseasoned timber and whilst this meant a shorter body life, London Transport went ahead. Delivered between April and November 1946, all the 100-strong Park Royal HGF-registered bodied buses went to the Sutton depot in south London.

By the early 1950s, as new RTs entered service in abundance, it was time for the London Daimlers to go. The chassis had plenty of life in them. Indeed, Belfast Corporation bought exactly 100 of the 281 London Daimler utilities and this included 13 of the Park Royal HGFs. After rebodying, Belfast used them until the end of the sixties. Southend Corporation also bought and rebodied 13 Daimlers, including five Park Royal HGFs, with other Daimlers finding their way to independent operators such as Trimdon Motor Services and Bee-Line, both in Durham. Southend, like Ledgard, wanted more. However, London Transport did not want to release further buses into the UK market. Therefore, many were exported to Ceylon who bought many Guy and Daimler utilities, including 36 of the Park Royal HGFs.

Ledgard bought 23 of the former 1946-built D-class Park Royal-bodied buses from the dealers Norths and they rebodied one as a single decker. Therefore, 22 double deckers entered service between 1953 and 1955 with their original Park Royal bodies. They had all been overhauled once in 1949 and then nine of them were overhauled again in 1952. However, in November 1952 London Transport decided not to overhaul any more. Therefore, when London's RTL class started to enter service at the Sutton depot in November 1953, those buses that had only been overhauled once were the first ones to be withdrawn and sold.

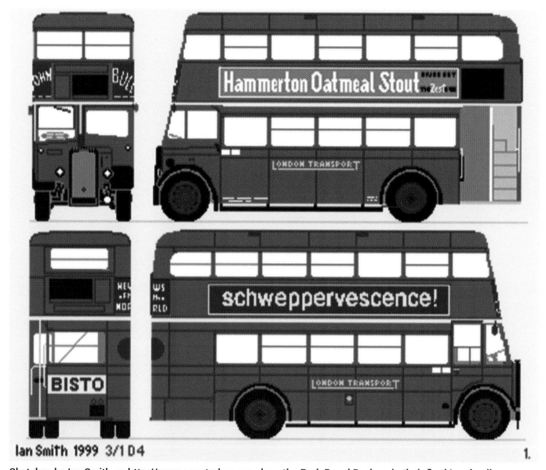

Ian Smith 1999 3/1 D 4   1.

Sketches by Ian Smith on http://www.countrybus.org show the Park Royal D-class in their final London livery.

The Daimlers Arrive

The Daimlers were bought by Ledgard for £350 each, below the advertised price of £450 but still giving a good return for Norths on the £165 they paid to London. The D-class buses were of variable mechanical quality because, as mentioned, the 1953 first buys were only overhauled once, in 1949. Ledgard, however, overhauled all of them at either their Armley (Leeds) or Otley depots, after which they then obtained a new certificate of fitness. Some of the bodies were not too good so the wooden framework received a lot of attention, along with some repanelling. Conversely, some HGFs bought for spares were found to be good, so they entered service.

The bodies had the normal London Transport destination layouts with three-window front and rear displays. However, like all the early post-war deliveries in London, only a part of the front via destination window was used at London.

Ledgard fully panelled over the rear destination indicators, with the side ones being retained and fitted with paper advertisements for their excursion and private hire activities.

Ledgard also rebuilt the front indicators and there were many variations. Eventually, the HGFs received the front Ledgard standard one-window indicators with some of these being fitted in a lower horizontal position. These Ledgard standard indicators were fitted between 1956 and 1958, when many also had the side half-drop windows replaced by sliding ones and also the upper opening drop-down front windows were replaced with one-pane glass. Not all had these changes and HGF910 still had half-drop windows on withdrawal.

Ledgard had 13 Park Royal HGFs enter service in 1953, eight in 1954 and two in 1955. The last two were intended for spares but were found to be good and replaced two of Ledgard's own 1944 Daimlers (JUA915 and 917) which were then used for spares. Additionally, one Duple-bodied HGF Daimler also came and will be seen later.

HGF897 entered service on 1 April along with HGF913, the first HGFs with Ledgard. Here it is seen at Otley on 9 May 1953 in another experimental livery variation with a dark blue lower waistband. As already explained, there were many livery experiments. (J S Cockshott)

Variations in Front Indicators

Ledgard changed the front indicators and there were three main variants found during the life of the HGFs. These variants were as follows:

1.0) Painted-over full indicators with a varied sized aperture left on the via window that had space for either one line or two or three lines. This remaining aperture was positioned high or in the middle. Some also had the Ledgard name painted on the intended top destination window. However, some did not.

A clean-looking HGF876 in 1954, soon after entering service in the 1953 livery with painted-over indicators. Some HGFs had paper sticker indicators, such was the need to get them into service. HGF876 is in Bradford, bound for Leeds. (J S Cockshott)

HGF954 with deeper blinds and white waistband.

HGF887 enters Otley in the 1955 livery with a green roof.

2.0) **Panelled-over indicators** that left an aperture showing either one line or two or three lines. In turn, the remaining aperture could be high, in the middle or at the bottom. Some had the Ledgard name at the top; some did not.

In its early days with Ledgard, HGF888 is seen at Bradford Chester Street on a snowy, wet and dirty day with a panelled-over indicator and no upper white band. It is parked on the side of the bus station that the Harrogate route departed from; the indicated Leeds route left from the other side of the bus station. (P M Photography)

HGF897 was the first HGF in service in 1953 and is seen here in later years at Troydale, leaving for Calverley. It has fixed upper front windows and the 1955 livery. (P M Photography)

HGF913 leaving Ilkley for Leeds via Otley with a slightly proud indicator panel.

HGF916 with no upper white band is on an evening peak to the Dyneley Arms on the Leeds to Otley road at the junction of the Bradford to Pool Bank and Harrogate road. (P M Photography)

HGF916 again, now missing the Ledgard name above the front indicator but sporting the white upper band of the 1955 livery. It was on a short working from Leeds to Pudsey on the Bradford route.

3.0) Standard indicators from 1955 used rubberised surrounds and these were mainly fitted in the middle with some being placed lower down. The front Ledgard name was no longer shown and, if needed, the upper front windows were replaced, with some buses received sliding saloon windows. 1955 also saw the introduction of the new livery with the green roof.

HGF891 at Ilkley depot with rear doors and retained half-drop windows. The rivets for the new destination are clearly seen as well as the advertising placed in the side indicator box. (J S Cockshott)

HGF891 in the 1955 livery with sliding saloon windows and fixed upper windows is parked up in Otley.

HGF954 heads towards the River Wharfe bridge in Otley from Newall on a local service.

Most buses went through all the types of indicators, initially with the rushed into service painted-over indicators, followed by panelling and finally with standard indicators. As seen, however, even with so-called standards, there were slight variations.

HGF953 and 908 in summer 1961 in Manchester, awaiting scrapping. 953 shows that not all the HGFs received standard indicators before their time was up. (J S Cockshott)

The HGFs never got to the post-1959 livery, apart from HGF805 that got close in 1957 with an experimental limited application of a light grey (or duck-egg blue) waistband, upper band and roof; the rest being dark blue, including the window surrounds. 805 was always different as it was the only Duple-bodied former London Daimler and had a single one-piece front indicator window from brand new. It was originally a Green Line bus and, therefore, painted green/white with black guards and a red-oxide roof. It had entered service at Romford for the 721/722 routes from London Aldgate via Stratford and Ilford, then the 721 via Romford to Brentwood and the 722 via Hornchurch to Upminster (Corbet's Tey). 805 stayed at Romford until August 1950 and was then painted red and returned to central area work at Merton (not far from Sutton), from where it was eventually withdrawn. The following pictures showcase HGF805's time with Ledgard.

HGF805 in its 1953 livery outside the Armley HQ.

HGF805 in the 1955 livery. (TLP)

In 1957, HGF805 received its last livery of two grey bands and a grey roof with the normal royal blue. 805 waits outside Leeds West Yorkshire Vicar Lane bus station for its turn on the joint route to Rawdon. (TLP)

The HGFs joined a variable fleet and the following images show the other double deckers that came after the HGFs.

1945 GYL291 new as LT D126 backs out of its stand at Vicar Lane. The Daimler CWA6, with Brush body acquired from Bee Line in Hartlepool in 1956, stayed until 1960 when it was scrapped.

In 1957 came XUG141, a Daimler CVG6 with Burlingham H63R body in the green-roof livery but with a lighter blue and custard banding; it was perhaps an unused demonstrator and a one-off. It is seen here on 7 April 1958 on a tea break in Ilkley. It eventually went to West Yorkshire as their DGW12. (J S Cockshott)

XUG141 in the 1959 livery at the Horsforth via Hawksworth Road terminus from Leeds. The terminus was shared with Leeds CT route 50 to Gipton.

XUG141 was soon followed by the 'famous six' from Roe which entered service in September 1957. These were AEC Regent Vs with Roe bodies and registered 1949 to 1954U. Brand-new AEC Regent V 1949U is at Roe's. (Geoff Lumb)

1949U on a trip from Leeds to Bradford. Otley had four of the six, and Leeds had the other two. (P M Photography)

The allocations to routes of these six buses were usually as follows:

- Leeds–Guiseley–Ilkley had three from Otley and one from Leeds; these four buses covered virtually all the mileage on the basic half-hourly service.
- Leeds–Otley–Ilkley used one bus from Otley on the hourly through service.
- Leeds–Pudsey–Bradford had the second Leeds vehicle.

It has been reported that a bus on the Leeds to Ilkley route would do eight return trips a day and this resulted in mileages per day of around 260 via Guiseley, whilst the one on the route via Otley did around 280 miles per day. This compares to the later low-bridge double-decker routes to Horsforth from Otley, where a Chevin bus did 220 miles a day and a White Cross bus 204 miles a day.

1951U in the 1959 livery at Park Place, Leeds, after King Street had become a one-way street in 1964. These new 1957 Regent Vs were to be the last new buses purchased, apart from a few coaches. Thereafter, only second-hand buses were acquired right up to the end when, in October 1967, Ledgard was bought by the Tilling Group's West Yorkshire Road Car Company (who had their main depots in Harrogate, York, Bradford, Keighley and Leeds). The entire batch of 1949 to 1954U was operated by West Yorkshire from 1967 to 1969 as their DAW5 to 10. (Geoff Lumb)

In 1957 came five 1944 Daimler CWA6 ex-Midland Red with Duple H56R bodies that were rebuilt by Willowbrook in 1951/1952. GHA968 is parked up in Park Place, Leeds, after running in from Bradford.

GHA936 and 941(below) were heavily rebuilt by Ledgard but only got a two-year certificate of fitness, which seemed to convince Ledgard not to do any more, considering the future expense of undertaking such work. Whilst 968 and 945 were withdrawn in 1960 and 965 in 1961, 941 went in December 1961, followed by 936 in May 1962.

EN8408 from Bury CT entered service with Ledgard in June 1959 and is seen in Bradford on 24 April 1960. With a 1952 Roe body on a 1946 chassis, it fitted in well with Ledgard with its Daimler CWA6 chassis. It must have been one of the last painted in the 1955 livery with a green roof, as the next buses (single deckers) were in the 1959 livery with grey roofs. (J S Cockshott)

In summer 1959 came five 1946 Albion CX13s with 1951 to 1953 BBW B35R bodies (they originally had Pickering bodies). They came from Red & White in 1959 to replace double deckers on the Bradford to Harrogate route. Registered EWO772/773, FAX 306, 308 and 311, three were allocated to Bradford, one was a spare at Otley and one went to Armley, but this one was often loaned to Bradford. They were the first buses to introduce the new blue/grey livery and had been renovated and repainted by Samlesbury in Preston from April 1959. 311 entered service in July 1959, 772/773 and 306 in August and 308 in September 1959. They were soon withdrawn due to bodywork issues, with 773 going last in 1962.

FAX308 waits outside Otley depot acting as a 'thunderbird'.

The end of the HGFs

By 1961, all the HGFs were withdrawn, apart from the last one in February 1962. This was also the same finishing time as the last of the 1943 to 1944 Guys and Daimlers, along with some of the 1945 Daimlers.

The replacements in 1960 were 15 newer Daimlers and one Leyland, and in 1961 came 16 Leylands and one Bristol K. These came from varied fleets.

In 1960, Ledgard bought ten 1948 Daimler CVD6/Brush H56Rs formerly operated by Leeds CT. These were registered LNW522 to 531. Thereafter, Leeds council banned the sale of buses to local operators as the councillors were unhappy over the selling of good buses to the competition. 528 to 531 entered service with Ledgard in January 1960, followed by 522 to 527 in August 1960. They were withdrawn between 1963 and 1965.

530 is inbound from Horsforth at Kirkstall. 529/530 were repainted by Maudslay of Leeds and the grey was not extended around to the driver's cab. All the others were repainted 'normally' by Salmesbury of Preston.

LNW526 leaves Chester Street to go across Morley Street and then past the Town/City Hall in the background. A Bradford FKY Regent/Weymann is approaching on the Great Horton Road routes and the Hebble behind is on the Halifax stand. (Geoff Lumb)

The ex-Leeds LNWs were followed by four very similar 1948 Daimler/Brush from Exeter CT. These were registered JFJ50 to 52 and 55. They entered service in July 1960 and were withdrawn in 1963.
   JFJ55 waits in Leeds on Cookridge Street. (Geoff Lumb)

Exeter JFJ51 entered service in July 1960 and is seen here in November 1960 in Chester Street bus station, Bradford, on the Harrogate route and on the other side of Chester Street from where Ledgard's Leeds route started. Some have erroneously reported the Harrogate route was a joint service with West Yorkshire. Far from it, Ledgard had their own service – West Yorkshire left on their route 53 to Harrogate at 25 and 55 minutes past the hour and Ledgard at 10 past the hour. The only condition for Ledgard using the West Yorkshire side was that the bus could not wait and park/load at the place shown in the photo but could only come on stand two minutes before departure. (J S Cockshott)

An unusual bus came in early 1961. SDU711 was a 1956 Daimler CVG6 demonstrator and Commercial Show attendee in 1956 and 1958 with a Willowbrook H66RD body.

SDU711 is on Wellington Street, likely coming from Armley depot to pick up a run to Otley from Cookridge Street. (Tony Greaves)

SDU711 has come from King Street into Wellington Street and is bound for Horsforth. Retained by West Yorkshire in 1967 as their DGW11, it ran for two years before being scrapped in November 1969.

1961 saw seven buses from Bristol OC enter service. These were Leyland PD1A or Bristol K6A/ K6B chassis with either ECW or Bristol bodies. The Leylands had been part of a Tilling order in 1947 for 150 as Bristol were too busy. Put into service in 1947/1948 with Bristol OC, they stayed at Ledgard until 1964/1967.

LAE2, a 1948 Leyland PD1A with its upright Bristol body, entered service in April 1961 and stayed for six years. Its tall angular body was not very pretty. Whilst within the maximum height of 14ft 6in, they were soon banned from the Leeds to Bradford route after the roof ventilators were scraped when running under a railway bridge on the outskirts of Leeds. Alongside is MUA862 at the temporary Bradford depot in Bairds TV yard, across the road from the Ledgard depot. LAE2 was withdrawn in January 1967 and sent for scrap. (TLP)

LAE12, new in 1948, entered service in February 1961 and was the first ECW-bodied vehicle. It is leaving Cookridge Street for Woodhouse Lane in Leeds. After withdrawal in April 1965, LAE12 had its seats removed and it was used at Otley for towing. It passed to West Yorkshire in 1967 and in early 1968 was earmarked for preservation, but with a defective engine and poor body it went for scrap. As a true survivor, it was not yet finished and its chassis went to Malta as the basis for a single-decker bus from the Dockyard and was known to be still running there in 1990.

KHW631 entered service in March 1961 and is working on the Otley local route from Newall, West Busk Lane, to Westbourne. It stayed until July 1967. (TLP)

KHY395 with a full radiator blanket at Cookridge Street, Leeds, also entered service in March 1961 and stayed to the end in October 1967. It finished via Norths in Sherburn, finally going to Parkers Bradford for scrap in April 1968.

KHY746 entered service in October 1961 and was a Bristol K6B that had 'escaped' the ban on selling on Bristol-engined buses. It is on the Ilkley to Leeds via Otley route and was an early withdrawal in August 1964 when it was decided not to extend its certificate of fitness for another three years, so it went for scrap.

Later in 1961 came 11 all Leylands. First into stock, in August, were four ex-Ribble PD1A/Leyland BCKs, new to Ribble in 1947, followed in November by two batches from Preston CT. These were three ARN 1946 PD1s with Alexander/Leyland bodies and four BCK 1947 PD1As with Leyland bodies, except BCK633 which was Samlesbury/Leyland. All were withdrawn in 1967.

   At the temporary depot at Bairds TV factory near to the Ledgard Bradford depot are, left to right, ex-Ribble BCK414 and Preston CT BCK624 and 636. The latter had slight variations in number plates and rubberised indicators. Unfortunately, all have blue painted radiators. (TLP)

Ex-Ribble BCK422 with silver radiator heading for Leeds from Ilkley/Otley. (Bus Photos UK)

Ex-Preston ARN393 and possibly BCK621 with Otley Chevin in the background. (TLP)

ARN392 on New Road Side, Horsforth, on the Ilkley via Guiseley route. Each ARN had different front destination treatment. (Tony Greaves)

Ex-Preston BCK621 outside the Otley depot on 12 August 1967 with a good display of A-boards.

BCK633 (with subcontracted Samlesbury body), on New Brook Street, Ilkley, is for Middleton Sanatorium that had three journeys a week on a Wednesday, Saturday and Sunday. 1953U behind is on the Leeds via Guiseley route and has yet to turn round lower down New Brook Street.

Rochdale's 1948 GDK401 to 405 came from Rochdale in March 1962. AEC Regent IIIs with East Lancashire H59R bodies, they soon had their side windows replaced in different styles as was often the case with Ledgard.

GDK401 had a heavy overhaul before it entered service and is seen on a private hire. It was the only one left in service when West Yorkshire took over in October 1967, but they did not operate it and sent it to their York depot for storage. It went to the dealers Norths in January 1968, and it finally went for scrapping two months later. (Bus Photos UK)

GDK404 on the Harrogate to Bradford route has passed Lister Park in Bradford and has around a mile to run. The rebuilt rubberised windows were fitted to 402 to 404 (and were similar to the ones on MUA861). (Tony Greaves)

GDK405 is in the temporary Bradford depot and has been working on the Acres Hall, Pudsey route to Calverley. It has been fitted with neat flush side windows, as was GDK401. (TLP)

Also in 1962 came two different buses from Felix Motors of Hatfield, Doncaster. Seen above is GWY157, an AEC Regent III with a Roberts H56R body from 1948. (Bus Photos UK)

The other bus from Felix was JWU131, a 1950 Leyland PD2/1 with Leyland H56R body, a type perfectly at home with Ledgard. Here, it is leaving Otley for Leeds.

Both GWY157 and JWU131 worked up to 1967 and were sold for scrap by West Yorkshire in 1968. (Tony Greaves)

In May 1963 came LHU520, Ledgard's only Bristol K5G with an ECWH56R body that was new in 1948. It went in January 1966 as it had come at the same time as the first ex-London RTs and was eclipsed by the RT's performance.

Bristol K5G meets K6B with Ledgard's LHU520 in Bradford Chester Street next to West Yorkshire DB21. Both buses would leave at 10 minutes past the hour. The West Yorkshire K6B would take 52 minutes to get to Otley, going on a circuitous route via Greengates and Yeadon, whilst Ledgard's K5G for Harrogate, via Otley, would take 45 minutes to get to Otley on a more direct route.

NXP864 was one of the first four RTs entered into stock in May 1953 and is being closely watched at Ilkley depot. (Neil Halliday)

MLL838 passes through Guiseley on a short from Leeds on the Ilkley route and will soon reach White Cross. Unusually, MLL838 has not yet been finished as the panelling over the roof box needs some paint. Between July and December 1963 another 18 RTs came into stock. (Tony Greaves)

There was little variation in the appearance of Ledgard's RTs and they did not have the variations and frills of the earlier HGFs. All looked the same, with rear indicators panelled over, the roof box, where fitted, removed and standard Ledgard front indicators. Minor body variations could, however, be seen with the fitting of the front standard indicators. The roof box RTs had a narrower covering panel, whereas the non-roof box bodies, with their full three split-indicator space, required a wider panel.

The mass standardisation on RT/RTLs continued and the last one was purchased for spares in January 1967. Overall, 43 came to Ledgard and three of these were used for spares. Obviously, Ledgard were impressed with the RT/RTL, as in 1965 two had come via Super of Upminster and three via Lesney Products of Ilford. Most were green Country area models, as these were preferred due to them having a higher rear axle drive, making them more suitable for Ledgard than red Central area models with the lower drive fitted, which were more suitable for stop/start work in slower moving traffic.

GTY169 was another one-off and came from Tyneside Omnibus, one of the Northern General companies, and was bought by Ledgard in August 1966. It entered service in December 1966 and was a 1954 Leyland PD2/12 with MCW Orion H59R body.

The last double deckers bought in 1966 were PDV726 and 732, which were purchased in September 1966 and placed in service in December 1966. Formerly with Devon General, Torquay, they were 1954 AEC Regent IIIs with Weymann Orion H58RD bodies.

PDV726 enters Armley depot yard and looks to have finished duty at Pudsey Troydale on the route from Calverley.

The last double deckers to enter service in January and March 1967 were MCY405/408 and NCY453/455 (seen above in Otley with West Yorkshire names). Ledgard seems to have caught the lightweight Orion bug as these AEC Regent Vs had the Weymann version and originated in 1955 and 1956 with South Wales Transport, Swansea. All four were soon to be taken into stock with West Yorkshire as their DAW1 to 4 and stayed until November 1969 when they went to Smith's Coaches in Reading. (Escrick Bus & Coach Archive)

Chapter 4

Ledgard and the Moorfield Routes

The two Otley to Horsforth routes and the buses that ran on them have an interesting story. Up to early 1959, pre-war Leyland single deckers were mainly found on the two routes. After 1959 came low-bridge Bristols from United and Bristol, followed by replacements from Ribble and London Transport.

The Moorfield routes came to Ledgard in January 1934 from the Moorfield Bus Company who were based in Yeadon (with the depot then being in the Rawdon local area). This company had started out in 1929 when they bought a shed/garage at Moorfield Drive from a local haulier called F & H Croft. Moorfield had a fleet of small petrol-engined, normal-control buses and operated excursions and stage services from Horsforth to Dean Head (a short, under 2-mile route that was later abandoned) along with the two Horsforth to Otley routes of around 8 miles each.

The purchase by Ledgard came with five (also reported as seven) petrol-engined buses in an orange and white livery. This livery soon went, and the buses were replaced by a variety of Ledgard's Leyland single deckers.

The Moorfield Buses

From the 1930s to 1959, the buses used by Ledgard were mainly Leyland TS single-decker cascaded coaches. Ledgard policy was to use coaches for ten years, then as buses for another five years. However, after 1959 the Moorfield routes became double decked. This was said to minimise duplication by the single deckers, as up to 16 single deckers had been based at Moorfield and these were replaced by eight to ten double deckers.

It has also been said that this single to double deck replacement was because the road under the former railway bridge on Henshaw Lane in Yeadon had been lowered in 1957 and thus low-bridge buses could now pass under the bridge. This suggestion, however, is rather strange as West Yorkshire had converted their former single-decked Bradford to Otley route 50, which also used Henshaw Lane, to low-bridge double deckers in 1953.

From 1959 came Bristols from United AS and Bristol OC and then, from 1963 until 1967, the ex-Ribble Leylands and ex-London RLH class AEC Regents. The Henshaw Lane bridge itself was finally demolished on 2 March 1969, after the demise of Ledgard.

The Bristols that came in 1959, finally, and sadly, saw off the last of the Leyland TSs – the 1937 EUG124 and 125 (that had been re-plated/rebodied), the 1938 CKW267 and the 1939 HUB499. These four were all withdrawn between February and July 1959.

Further details on the buses used in post-war years at Moorfield follow.

KY7082 from 1934 was an ex-B & B Bradford, a company taken over by Ledgard in 1935. It was a Leyland LT5B that was re-engined with a Gardner 5LW engine in 1946, but it did not re-enter service until after being rebodied with an ex-East Yorkshire ECW body in September 1954. It is outside Moorfield depot at Yeadon with an engineless Bedford OWB behind. It was withdrawn in October 1956 but stayed in public service as a restroom for a minicab firm in Nottingham until 1961. (J S Cockshott)

In 1935 came two all Leyland TS7s that were later rebodied. BUA 402 is seen here with its original 1935 Leyland body outside Otley depot.

BUA402 is seen here in an experimental light and dark blue livery with an ex-Bullocks of Wakefield Barnaby body that was fitted in 1952.

BUA402 turns into Otley bus station. It was withdrawn in 1958.

1935 Leyland TS7 BUA403 originally had the same body as BUA402 and is seen here at Otley in July 1953, just after being rebodied with an ECW body from an East Yorkshire bus (like KY7082 on page 52) in May 1953. It was withdrawn in 1957. (J S Cockshott)

In 1936 came six Leyland TS7s with EEC coach bodies with CUG/AKW registrations. Similar to contemporary Ribble coaches, they served Ledgard well. CUG842 is seen here in a bodybuilders photograph in the coach livery of blue, black and cream. After ten years as a coach, it went to Moorfield for ten years until its withdrawal in 1957. (David Beilby, The GEC Collection)

AKW849 is a 1936 sister to CUG842 but is in the B & B Tours of Bradford livery. It was delivered in B & B's red, turquoise and cream livery but after 1945, B & B vehicles were painted in Ledgard's normal livery. 849 is believed to have been the last one in B & B livery and it served at Moorfield from the late 1940s until its withdrawal in December 1956 when, like CUG842, it went to the contractor Yorkshire Hennebique in Leeds from where both were scrapped in 1961. The unusual porch door on a coach may be noted. This was a specific Ledgard specification to make it easier to use them as service buses after they had served ten years as a coach. (David Beilby, The GEC Collection)

AKW849, now in Ledgard stage bus livery with the light blue relief that replaced the former cream band/stripe. It is shown at Otley bus station in October 1956 and had just two months to go before withdrawal. (J S Cockshott)

A nearside view of CUG845, which was the last of the six 1936 Tigers to be withdrawn in October 1957. The author well recalls a bus like this being brought home by a Moorfield driver to show it off to his family at Greengates in Bradford. This involved around a 5-mile round trip away from a normal Ledgard route, so the driver's name had better remain a secret. (P M Photography)

Five more Leyland TS7s arrived in 1937 and were registered EUG/BKW with Duple bodies. It was planned that they would be rebodied in 1954 with second-hand ECW bodies. However, EUG126, seen here at Yeadon Fountain, was found to be in good condition and kept its body. (J S Cockshott)

In late 1954, the 1937 Duple bodies on EUG124 to 126 were felt to be deteriorating so they were taken out of service in October 1954 and joined EUG127 at Moorfield. 127 had been in storage since 1947, its body having been removed/scrapped, and the chassis stored.

In November 1954, four 1939 Leyland TS8s with ECW DP32F bodies were bought from Norths ex-United, the bodies being rebuilt in 1951 by Willowbrook. The reports vary on whether the Ledgard 1954/1955 exercise was about rebodying or registration replacement. What is clear is that the four ex-United TS8s that were bought were registered EHN 965 to 967/970, and also when EUG126 was fully examined, it was found to be acceptable and so it was returned to service. So now, one United bus was surplus; consequently, EHN965 was cannibalised for spares and the remains scrapped.

For the other buses, the question is, were they rebodied or re-plated? The following shows three varied opinions reported in the literature:

Registration plate	Source 1	Source 2	Source 3
EUG124	Registration plates put on 967.	Rebodied with body from 966.	Rebodied with body from 967.
EUG125	Registration plates put on 970.	Rebodied with body from 967.	Rebodied with body from 970.
EUG127	Registration plates put on 966.	Registration plates put on 970.	Registration plates put on 966.

What is sure is that there were now three Leyland TSs with ECW bodies and EUG126 retained its original Duple body.

EUG124, seen here with its second-hand ECW body that was rebuilt by Willowbrook in 1950/1951, was one of the last single deckers withdrawn at Moorfield in June/July 1959.

In 1938, four more Leyland TS7s with Duple bodies came with GUA/CKW registrations. These were withdrawn in 1956/1957 with CKW267 being the last one in 1959.
   GUA637 is parked up opposite the bus station in Otley.

In 1939, with HUB registrations, came two Leyland TS8s with Duple bodies. HUB499 was rebuilt in 1952 by Rhodes of Bingley. Intended as a pilot for potential other rebuilds, the exercise was, however, considered to be too expensive.

Seen in November 1954 in Otley, HUB499 was one of the last single deckers withdrawn at Moorfield in June/ July 1959. (J S Cockshott)

Between 1943 and 1945 came five Bedford OWBs with Roe or Duple bodies and JNW/JUA registrations. JNW347 rests at Moorfield and was withdrawn in July 1953. (J S Cockshott)

An ex-Daimler demonstrator with Duple B36D body from 1951 and bought in 1956, LRW377 is parked up in Bradford Chester Street bus station off the Harrogate route in September 1958. It was an unhappy bus that was initially at Otley for a year, from where it may have strayed onto the Horsforth routes. It was next transferred to Bradford in 1957, from where it was withdrawn three years later. (Roy Marshall/Omnibus Society)

Next came four buses with the acquisition of Kitchin & Sons' stage route in April 1957. Ledgard got Kitchin's two routes from Calverley to Pudsey on the western outskirts of Leeds and were to convert them to double-decker operation. As part of the deal, Ledgard gave in exchange their excursion and tours licences from Pudsey which Kitchin continued with until they were acquired by Wallace Arnold in January 1959.

JJW239 was the oldest of the four buses from Kitchin & Sons. It was a Guy Arab III with a Guy B35F body built in 1948 and was a former Guy demonstrator with the registration GUY3 until 1951, when it went to a company in Burnley before coming to Kitchin in May 1952. It is seen here at the Horsforth terminus ready for a return to Otley. It was first allocated to Moorfield but the double-decker invasion saw it transferred for a short time to Armley before it went to Bradford for the Harrogate route. It was withdrawn in 1961 after an unfortunate and freak accident in Harrogate bus station. (J S Cockshott)

GUY3 was an ex-demonstrator Guy Arab UF with a Guy (Park Royal frame) B40F body dating from 1950. This bus was Guy's prototype under-floor-engined bus exhibited at the 1950 Earls Court Show. It was another ex-Kitchin bus and is shown here leaving Otley at the junction of Boroughgate and Kirkgate with the driver alongside Weegmans butchers, pork pie maker extraordinaire. GUY3 was purchased by Kitchin & Sons, Pudsey, in 1956, entered service in March 1957 and then came to Ledgard in April 1957. GUY3 spent most of its time at Moorfield and a few years at Bradford depot. In 1963, it was repanelled and reseated to B42F. It stayed with Ledgard until the end and was sold by West Yorkshire to Norths from where it was sold on for scrap. (TLP)

NWW805, here turning into Otley bus station on a Bradford to Harrogate duty from Bradford depot, was one of two unusual Atkinson PL745H with a Burlingham B44F body bought new by Kitchin & Sons in 1954. Twin NWW806 was at Moorfield for a short time and then both NWW805/806 finished their time at Bradford on the Harrogate route. Both were withdrawn in November 1963. 805 saw further bus work with Wood of Mirfield and Beresford's of Cheddleton and finally as a builder's storage shed, before being scrapped in 1989. 806 worked for Garners, Bridge of Weir, until being withdrawn in 1969. (TLP)

In 1959 double deckers were purchased for Moorfield and in came five Bristol K6As with ECW bodies from United Automobile Services, Darlington. These buses had the high bonnet line that was used on Bristol Ks from 1937 to 1946 and the bodies differed as follows:

- GHN631 and 838 had the standard ECW 55 seat body with flush fitting windscreen and straight horizontal lower deck front window.
- GHN635, 837 and 840 were built for Leyland TD2s that had a shorter wheelbase. Therefore, when fitted onto the K chassis, the capacity was two seats fewer. They had a sloping front windscreen and short front upper and lower bays, as well as a sloping lower deck front window.

All entered service in the mainly blue livery with green roofs, and on first repaint they received the blue/grey livery that was introduced later in 1959. In typical Ledgard style, each had unique front indicators.

GHN631, as it was when it entered service, loads in Otley with an ex-London D-class HGF behind.

GHN631, now in the late 1959 livery, still clearly shows the former United name glass, which had been painted black, above the registration number. 631 was the first GHN to be withdrawn in March 1964. (Roy Marshall)

GHN635 with sloping windscreen loads at Otley on a wet day. It was the last to be withdrawn in July 1965.
(John L May OTA)

GHN837 has 'gained' this small indicator on being repainted (and fortunately was the only one so treated).
(Roy Marshall)

GHN838 is shown with a different style of indicator and with no United name glass at the front (as the registration number plate covered it). (P M Photography)

GHN840 is in the original into service livery with high-placed fleet name and a sign advertising 'Ledgards Luxury Coaches'. It is also helping out Otley depot on the Leeds route; Moorfield did occasionally loan buses to Otley depot.

1947 Bristol K6A KHU602 and 603 entered service in December 1959, by which time the blue/grey livery was the new standard. They were Bristol Omnibus Company with ECW bodies, respectively having Bristol K6A and K6B chassis. 602 is loading in Otley in May 1962 and served until January 1967, longer than the other KHUs. (Roy Marshall)

New in 1948, KHU608 came in May 1961 and loads up at Otley in May 1962 whilst being propped up by a conductor. It was withdrawn before its contemporaries as it developed a cracked chassis. KHW243 behind was an ex-Bristol OC Leyland PD1A with Bristol H56R body new in 1947. Both came to Ledgard in 1961. (Roy Marshall)

EUH959 came in 1963 from Eynon and was originally with Western Welsh, hence the BET-style destination screen. It was Ledgard's first Leyland PD2/3 with Leyland low-bridge body and was new in 1950. On a wet and dirty day, EUH959 loads in Otley for Horsforth. (TLP)

In February and June 1964 came four 1950 all Leylands from Ribble (CRN852/855/866 and DRN273). DRN273 was the only one with rear doors. (John L May OTA)

Between December 1964 and February 1965 came four ex-London RLH AEC Regents with Weymann L53R bodies, new in 1950, KYY502/4/6/8.

KYY504 is at Yeadon Town Hall, heading back to Otley.

KYY506 makes its way back to Otley. Both the ex-London RTs and the RLHs were popular buses with drivers, and the RLHs were said to be preferred over the ex-Ribble Leyland PD2s at Moorfield depot. (Harry Luff OTA)

The final Moorfield main working allocation was four buses from London Transport and four from Ribble. CRN852 was, however, parked up in August 1967 with front brake problems.

In 1966 came two 1947 Leyland PD1s from Ribble. They had been rebodied in 1955 by Burlingham to replace the former Brush bodies. Intended as spare buses for Moorfield, both BCK427/441 were 'un-needed' purchases as their low-bridge bodies were not routinely needed at Moorfield. They mainly found themselves at Bradford where the rear doors were useful for the Harrogate route.

BCK427 is seen in the paint shop.

The Routes

Otley is a traditional market town on the banks of the River Wharfe, some 10 miles north-west of Leeds and 10 miles north-east of Bradford. The town was developed on the south bank of the River Wharfe, but in the 20th century, Otley expanded to the north of the river to include new developments at Newall and the Weston Estate and the population grew to around 14,000 people.

A grit-stone escarpment called the Chevin dominates the south side of the valley, a part of this escarpment being the Chevin Forest Park. Historically, the Chevin was quarried; the foundation stones for the Houses of Parliament came from Otley Chevin and, coincidentally, Guy Fawkes, the attempted destroyer of the Houses of Parliament, was a Yorkshireman. The owners of Farnley Hall on the outskirts of Otley are the Fawkes family, who are distantly related to Guy Fawkes.

The Chevin is just under 1,000ft high and beyond the Chevin, towards Leeds, is Horsforth, some 8/9 miles away by road from Otley (and then another 5 miles into Leeds). As a suburb of Leeds, Horsforth is on the Leeds to York via Harrogate railway line and is close to Leeds Bradford Airport, where the former Moorfield route to Dean Head skirts the runway.

Between Otley and Horsforth are Guiseley and Yeadon, both with a current population of around 22,000 people each. Guiseley had Crompton Parkinson as a major employer until its factory closed in 2004 and was also the home of Silver Cross prams from 1936 to 2002. The town is also known as the origin of the Harry Ramsden's fish and chip shops; the restaurant is still there at White Cross but is now with a different company called the Wetherby Whaler.

Yeadon grew out of Guiseley and was a centre for woollen manufacturing. It is now very close to Leeds Bradford Airport, where the airline Jet2 has its headquarters.

The area today is effectively living accommodation for people commuting into Leeds and, to a lesser degree, into Bradford. Guiseley has branch railway lines with a frequent train service connecting Ilkley, Bradford and Leeds.

The two Ledgard routes from Otley to Horsforth ran every hour and each route had a 55-minute journey time so, during normal operations, two buses per route were required. In the early to mid-1950s Moorfield had an allocation of between 14 and 16 single deckers, with two others at Otley; this shows the high degree of duplication that was required at peak times.

When the routes were double decked, Moorfield depot had an allocation of between eight and ten double deckers. Four were required to operate the normal service and the others used for peaks, school extras and maintenance cover. It was also not unknown for Moorfield to support Otley depot with double deckers at busy times, so these could occasionally be seen on Otley depot routes to Leeds and Ilkley as well as on the Otley local routes.

Moorfield Routes Descriptions

This route description follows the bus journey from Otley to Horsforth. As it uses images to illustrate the points passed, some buses are outbound from Otley, whilst others are inbound.

Ex-Bristol KHU602 swings into Otley bus station with a full load and blind set for the outbound journey.

Ex-United GHN840 in the dark blue and green roof livery is seen not long after entering service and is well loaded at Otley. 840 has an unusually high placed Samuel Ledgard name transfer on the side. It was the third GHN to enter service in 1959 and was to be eventually replaced by an ex-London RLH in 1965. (Roy Marshall)

A rare event for these coaches, as they were never normally used, LUB676 is in Otley loading for Horsforth on 12 January 1958. A batch of eight delivered in 1948 and the last with a porch-style door, they were clearly intended for stage work in their later life. Leyland PS1s with Duple bodies were rebuilt between 1952 to 1954 by Samlesbury with full fronts to make them look more modern. (J S Cockshott)

Originally, the route had left Otley along the rather steep and narrow West Chevin Road, directly to the Chevin Inn. However, this direct route was stopped in 1947 when a landslip closed the road and the longer 'in the valley bottom' route on Bradford Road was then used.

Ex-United Bristol GHN837 was the last GHN to enter service in July 1959 and is seen a month later. It is running out of Otley on Bradford Road, with the Westbourne estate on the left of the picture. The A65 junction is about a mile away at the, then called, Fox & Hounds pub. (J S Cockshott)

GHN837, in the later livery, is on Bradford Road going into Otley (and is chasing another bus which can be seen on the horizon) with GHN635 which is heading for Horsforth. (Omnicolour)

KHU608 leaves Otley on Bradford Road. (TLP)

After about 2 miles on Bradford Road, having run past the Westbourne Estate, the route comes to the junction with the A65, which runs from Leeds, past Horsforth, Yeadon and Guiseley, into Ilkley and Skipton, then on to Settle, Ingleton, Kirkby Lonsdale and finishes in Kendal, Cumbria.

GHN837 is passing under the bridge that once carried the railway to Ilkley. (Omnicolour)

GHN635 is climbing up out of the valley for Horsforth and has just passed the Butlers scrapyard. It will soon arrive at the Fox & Hounds pub. (TLP)

GHN635, in the earlier blue and green roof livery, is on the Fox & Hounds roundabout. The A65 is on the left towards Ilkley. (TLP)

At the junction with the A65 at the Fox & Hounds pub (now called just the Fox), the buses would turn left towards Leeds. The A65 was an important road used by Ledgard buses as, besides the Moorfield routes, the following frequent services ran on parts of the A65:

- Leeds (King St), Guiseley to Ilkley, every 30 minutes; this route ran directly on the A65 for virtually the entire journey.
- Bradford, White Cross and Menston (both on the A65), for Otley and on to Harrogate, every 60 minutes.
- Leeds (Vicar Lane), Headingley, West Park, Horsforth to Rawdon (on the A65), every 30 minutes, joint with West Yorkshire.

The Horsforth buses continued along the A65 from the Fox & Hounds to the Hare & Hounds pub at Menston Lane End, where the routes diverted for a few miles. The longer route turned left into Buckle Lane via West Chevin (the place the original route from Otley went directly to) for around 1.5 miles, and the shorter route ran for about 1 mile, going straight along the A65 via White Cross (where the Bradford to Harrogate service joined the A65).

Ex-Exeter JFJ50 crosses the Ilkley to Leeds and Bradford railway line at Menston, halfway between the Fox & Hounds and the Hare & Hounds. At the Hare & Hounds it will run into Menston village, before reversing and coming back to continue its journey to Bradford from Harrogate. (TLP)

KHU603 at West Chevin. It has come up Buckle Lane from the Hare & Hounds pub and is turning right for the bus stop. Ilkley Moor is on the horizon. (TLP)

KYY506 at the bus stop at West Chevin. The old route came here direct from Otley, using the road to the right, behind KYY506.

Both Horsforth routes originally would meet up again near Guiseley at the Kirk Lane/New Road (A65) junction and then continue on the A65/New Road to go up Henshaw Lane and into Yeadon for the Town Hall.

The route between Guiseley and Yeadon, however, had various changes over the years. For example, the Chevin route ran through the new Shaw Estate from December 1958 and then turned right to come back to the A65 to re-join the White Cross buses via Henshaw Lane to Yeadon. From June 1962, however, the Chevin route turned left from Shaw Estate and went more directly to Yeadon Town Hall.

CRN855 on Shaw Estate, bound for Otley. (Bus Photos UK)

At the halfway point and Otley bound, KHU603, a 1947 Bristol K6B from Bristol OC that entered service in January 1960, is at Yeadon Town Hall. It was very similar to the West Yorkshire K6Bs (their DB class) that ran on their route 50 from Bradford and which paralleled the Ledgard Horsforth route from Rawdon, through Yeadon and via White Cross into Otley. (Bus Photos UK)

CUG843 on Yeadon High Street opposite the Town Hall, with a Leeds double decker on a private hire behind (perhaps it was there for the Yeadon air show).

DRN273 is on Yeadon High Street, opposite the Town Hall, and has terminated there.

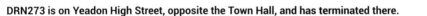

All Leyland EUH959 is halfway up the High Street in Yeadon by the Albert Inn.

After running up Yeadon High Street to Yeadon Fountain and Moorfield Mills, and turning right, the Moorfield depot was passed just after starting down the hill towards Rawdon and then back again, onto the A65. (From October 1950 to June 1957 the White Cross buses also had a small diversion into the Larkfield Estate between the depot and Rawdon.)

GHN838, after running a short from Otley to Yeadon, is at the top of Yeadon High Street by Yeadon Fountain and Moorfield Mills and is turning right onto the A658 Bradford/Harrogate road. In less than 100 yards it will be at the Moorfield depot. Another GHN is in the background heading for Otley. (TLP)

KHU602 struggles through the snow from Yeadon Fountain and is just above the Moorfield depot with the Peacock pub on the left (the large peacock emblem on the roof apex can just be seen).

The last Moorfield buses were ex-London RLHs and KYY504 makes its way from Horsforth to Otley. It is opposite the Stone Trough pub and will soon climb up to Yeadon Fountain and Moorfield Mills, passing the Moorfield depot. (Geoff Lumb)

On the A65, the Horsforth route joined the Rawdon via Horsforth and West Park route to Leeds, a joint Ledgard/West Yorkshire route running every 30 minutes. With the Horsforth buses, this gave four buses an hour between Rawdon to Horsforth (Old Ball) on the 9/10-minute journey.

Ex-Ribble CRN852 is seen in October 1964 at Rawdon and has just re-joined the A65, having come down from Yeadon on the road seen in the background to the right. At this junction, on the left, was the terminus of the Ledgard route to Rawdon, which was shared with West Yorkshire, which ran from Leeds via Headingley, West Park, and Horsforth. (P M Photography)

In addition, on this section of the A65 ran the Leeds to Ilkley buses that stayed directly on the A65. Rawdon junction (or Rawdon Coop to give the official name) was virtually the halfway point for the Ilkley route.

The Horsforth buses would soon, however, turn off left up the A65 to Over Lane, going on to Brownberrie Lane.

GHN840, with the sloping windscreen, is on Brownberrie Lane coming from Horsforth towards Rawdon for Otley. It is pictured in the as entered service condition, and with its unusually high-placed fleet name. It would later receive the blue/grey livery and then lose the high-placed fleet name. (P M Photography)

Soon, Horsforth (Old Ball) is reached, and at this roundabout by the Old Ball pub, buses from Otley turned right and stopped at the top of Long Row.

The routes diverged after Horsforth Old Ball/Long Row, with the West Chevin buses now going on the shorter route to the terminus. They ran for about 1 mile by turning left from Long Row onto Broadgate Lane and past the Ledgard Leeds to Horsforth via Hawksworth Road terminus at Stanhope Drive.

In January 1957, GUA638 is at the top of Long Row in Horsforth, opposite the Queens Arm pub and just a few yards on the left from the Old Ball pub and roundabout. The bus stop/terminus was also shared with the Wallace Arnold-owned (from 1952) Farsley Omnibus Company, which ran a frequent 5-mile-long service from Horsforth (Old Ball) to Pudsey from 1952 to 1968. (J S Cockshott)

Ledgard's EN8408 is at the Horsforth Stanhope Drive terminus with a Leeds Corporation AEC/Roe, that has also turned there on its route 50, behind it. (TLP)

GHN631 at the Horsforth terminus ready for its return to Otley.

The West Chevin buses then continued on Broadgate Lane to its junction with Low Lane (near to the former terminus until 1957 at the Woolpack). Here, they made a left turn onto Low Lane and after 400 metres they came to the Horsforth (Springfield Mount) terminus, completing the 8-mile route.

Meanwhile, the White Cross buses reached Horsforth (Springfield Mount) from Long Row on a longer 1.5-mile route. They went past Broadgate Lane and carried on to Town Street and Fink Hill and then right onto the Ring Road to meet up again with the A65. Here, they turned left at the roundabout before, again, leaving the A65 by turning left up Sunnybank Avenue, then on to Featherbank Avenue and then right onto the Ring Road again before soon making a left turn onto Wood Lane to its junction with Broadgate Lane. Here, the White Cross buses re-joined the West Chevin buses and went on to complete their 8-mile route.

From May 1947 to October 1959, the Chevin buses had run a circular route from Horsforth Old Ball, via Station Road and Troy Road, into Low Lane, going past Springfield Mount and the Woolpack (the former terminus up to early 1957) and, then, into Broadgate Lane to Long Row and back to the Horsforth Old Ball.

KHU608 has come from Horsforth and is at the A65 roundabout after coming along the A65 from Sunnybank Avenue. It will turn right at the roundabout and will run up where the traffic is in the background before soon turning left for Fink Hill and Town Street, then past the church (seen on the left horizon) and on to the Old Ball in Horsforth just after that. (Tony Greaves)

KYY508 has just left the Horsforth terminus and is on the top half of Low Lane.

KYY506 is turning off the top half of Low Lane into Broadgate Lane and will continue from there to Long Row on the shorter Chevin route to Horsforth Old Ball. (P M Photography)

From the bottom of Low Lane came the Ledgard route from Leeds via the A65, Kirkstall and Hawksworth Road, that had a headway of 30 minutes. The route from Leeds to Horsforth now paralleled the Otley-bound buses along Broadgate Lane. The White Cross buses soon went left on Wood Lane, whilst the Chevin buses carried on, on Broadgate Lane, for about half a mile to where the route from Leeds turned around at Horsforth (Stanhope Drive). After here, the Chevin route continued along Broadgate Lane to Long Row and Horsforth Old Ball.

Also using Low Lane was another 30-minute Ledgard headway route that was joint with West Yorkshire. This came from Leeds via Headingley, West Park, Butcher Hill and Horsforth and finished at Rawdon; this route ran the full length of Low Lane into Horsforth for the Old Ball roundabout.

Although the two Moorfield Otley routes were around 8 miles, the Chevin route was about half a mile longer. Indeed, crews also reckoned the White Cross was an easier shift with time to spare and were commonly waiting for time at the Old Ball, the Emmott Arms in upper Rawdon, Yeadon Town Hall, Guiseley Towngate and White Cross.

The buses were worked hard as a full-shifted Chevin bus did 220 miles a day and a White Cross bus covered 204 miles a day. This compares to the Leeds to Ilkley route that used the new AEC Regents 1949–1954U that could do eight return trips a day, resulting in mileages per day of around 260 via Guiseley, whilst those on the route via Otley did around 280 miles per day.

Chapter 5

Coaches

CUB1 from 1935 was exhibited at the 1935 Commercial Show and was a Maudslay SF40 with a Brush C36C body; the engine was replaced in 1947 with a Leyland diesel. Withdrawn in 1951, the chassis was scrapped in 1954, but in 1953 the body, after rebuilding by Rhodes in Bingley, went on Daimler JUB649 (now with the registration HGF948).

Other coaches came in service from 1936 (Leyland TSs registered CUG, EUG, GUA and HUB – these are covered in the section on the Moorfield bus route from Otley to Horsforth, see page 51). In 1948 came eight LUB/FAK registered Leyland PS1s with Duple bodies. LUB672 is seen on New Victoria Street, Bradford, probably on its way to either the Chester Street bus station or to the nearby excursion loading place on Morley Street.

The LUB/FAKs were rebuilt by Samlesbury between 1952 and 1954 with full fronts to make them look more modern. LUB675 was slightly different, having a straight non-curved bottom windscreen. In 1958, after ten years of coach work and with porch doors, these buses were ready to work as Moorfield buses. However, it changed to double-deck operation in 1959, but some were allocated to Moorfield from time to time. They were withdrawn in 1962/1964. (Peter Sykes collection from OTA)

New in 1949/1950 were six MUA registered Fodens with Plaxton bodies. Four were half cabs (863, 864, 867 and 868) and two had full fronts (865/866). All were withdrawn in 1966/1967.
   MUA 868 and 865 are seen near to Lisbon Street, Leeds, which was used on Saturdays as an overflow area for the nearby express bus station on Wellington Street. (Omnicolour)

Considered the flagship for some years, ONW2 was a 1951 Foden PVFE6 with Plaxton FC37F body. ONW2 is shown in a Plaxton official photograph in Scarborough. It went for preservation in 1968 but was scrapped after a major engine failure in 1970. It stayed at Ledgard until the end in 1967.

Six brand-new coaches were purchased in 1955, UUA791/2 AEC Reliance MU3RV and Leyland PSUC1/2's UUA793 to 796. All had the stylish Burlingham Seagull bodies with UUA791/2 and 796 having C41F bodies and 793 to 795 C41C. Used to successfully promote excursion and tour work, they ran often on hire to West Yorkshire Road Car if there was no 'own work'. Indeed, Ledgard often hired out their coaches, whilst hiring in from other operators to cover their own work.

UUA791 shows well the original blue and black colours in a painting by John Kinsley. (transport-art-collections.co.uk)

After the 1955 success with excursion and tours business, this activity was expanded and in 1956 more coaches were needed. After a visit to Lancashire Motor Traders the first came in August 1956 and were two AEC Regal IIIs, JP7865 and 8146, with unusual Beccols FC33F bodies from Smith's in Wigan. Originally with half cabs, they were rebuilt in 1951/1952 by Samlesbury, a company Ledgard also used.

JP7865 is seen in the blue and black coach livery, without fleet names. (TLP)

JP8146 and with fleet name. (TLP)

Also in August 1956, from Lancaster Motor Traders came two Leylands from two different companies in Oldham. FBU77 was a 1949 PS1/1 with a Plaxton C33F body, and FBU896 was a 1950 PS2/3 with a Burlingham C33F body. These completed the 1956 purchases.

   FBU77 in June 1957 is on hire to West Yorkshire and loading across Morley Street from the normal bus station. FBU77 left Ledgard in 1960 and then worked with a contractor until it was scrapped in 1963. (J S Cockshott)

FBU896 worked until March 1964 and was sold to Jackson, Bradford, for scrap in 1965.

In March 1957 came MTJ357, a Maudslay Regal IV with Burlingham Seagull C41C body that was new in 1951 to Robinson in Great Harwood and then went to Mascot in Norwich. It had a similar sliding centre door to Ledgard's own 1955 Leyland Seagulls, registered UUA793 to 795. With Ledgard until November 1963, it went to Hutchinson Brothers of Husthwaite, north of York, and was accidented in January 1969. (TLP)

Arriving in March 1957 from Baxter's of Airdrie was KUP949, a Leyland PS1/1 with Burlingham C33F body from 1950 and new to Iveson in the North East. It is seen here in Stanningley on private work. After arriving at Otley depot, KUP949 spent a few weeks at Yeadon before settling at Armley for the rest of its career. After the West Yorkshire takeover, KUP949 went on to be famous in restoration, especially the second time around when it also made a magnificent appearance at the Ledgard 50-year celebrations in 2017. (Tony Greaves)

New in 1951, this Leyland PSU1/11 with Duple C41F body was new to Baxter's of Airdrie and to Ledgard in April 1957. GVA289 spent its time with Ledgard until 1967, mainly at Bradford on coachwork. It is seen here reversing into the Hebble Walnut Street depot in Halifax and was probably on hire to Hebble. Withdrawn in 1967, it went on to further service as a staff bus with Lindley, metal fabricators in Queensbury, Bradford. (P M Photography)

In April 1957, a 1949 AEC Regal type rebuild with Burlingham C33F body came into the fleet, registered FJW938, and was followed in May 1957 by another bus from Smith's in Wigan, registered JP7221.

FJW938 operated until 1960 and worked for a contractor before being scrapped.

In May 1957 came JP7221 with a 1952 Bellhouse Hartwell FC33F body on a 1948 Leyland PS1/1 chassis Regal that had originally had a Pearson of Liverpool body, and had been rebuilt in 1955 to full front by Samlesbury in Preston. It did not stay for long and was withdrawn at the end of 1958 after an accident. It was salvaged for spares and the remains were scrapped in July 1960. It is seen on 10 August 1957 on hire to West Yorkshire in Bradford and loading on Chester Street, but across Morley Street from the bus station. Ledgard's Bradford depot manager, Tommy Kent, looks on. (J S Cockshott)

April 1960 brought KBU880, a 1955 Bedford SBO with Duple C38F body, new to Healings of Oldham and then to three other operators all in 1959! With Ledgard until November 1963, it passed, again, through three other operators until 1970. KBU880 is shown in June 1960 outside Otley depot. (J S Cockshott)

In April 1960 came GBU537 and 539 from Dyson of Hollingwood, Oldham. They were Leyland PS2/3s from 1951 with Plaxton FC39F bodies, as on ONW2. After accident damage to GBU539 in April 1963, the body was found to be rotten and so GBU537 was also withdrawn in November 1963. The bodies were sent to Blamires in Bradford and the chassis of 539 was rebuilt to Leyland PD2/37 standard for eventual rebodying. 537 was similarly started but was not completed as a suitable bodybuilder could not be found. The chassis remained at Armley before going for scrap in October 1967.

GBU537 is just past the Express bus station on Wellington Street, Leeds, with an 'On hire to West Yorkshire' sticker; the driver has likely gone to check where he is required.

In 1963, Ledgard bought eight 1954 Guy Arab LUFs with Picktree C35F bodies that were with Northern General. Registered DCN831 and 834 to 840, they came to Ledgard in January, February and April and entered service in April 1963. Seven stayed until the end; indeed it was rumoured that West Yorkshire were to rebody them with ECW bus bodies. However, 831 was dismantled for spares in February 1967 and the remains scrapped. 834 to 840 went to Norths, from where four went to a contractor in Mansfield and two went to a contractor working on the North Sea gas pipeline in Yorkshire. The one left at Norths went for scrap in 1968 and was followed by the other six in 1969. DCN832 came from Woods of Pollington in April 1966 and, like 831, was dismantled for spares.

DCN836 is seen above in its original classic livery at Morley Street, Bradford, with A-board excursion advertising. (TLP)

On 3 August 1963, DCN831 and 838, bound for Whitby and on hire to West Yorkshire, are loading at Saville Street, the overflow from Wellington Street coach station that was used on summer Saturdays. It was their first summer season with Ledgard. This 'new' livery had been applied through the summer of 1963 and removed the black. (J S Cockshott)

DCN839 at Halifax on hire to Hebble; the destination blind is a mistake. The new sky blue and ivory coach livery was introduced in February 1964. 839 has lost its front grill covers. (TLP)

In March 1963 came two Fords with Duple Yeoman C41F bodies. 8848WY from Waterhouse in Crawshawbooth near Rossendale was registered in 1961 in West Yorkshire by Hughes, dealers, who had also supplied 252BNW to Rogers of Leeds in 1962. Both went to West Yorkshire in 1967.

8848 is next to an excursion A-Board outside Otley depot on 25 May 1963 and advertising two excursions on 26 May, one at 0930 hours to Morecambe and to Bridlington at 1230 hours. (J S Cockshott)

In 1964, Ledgard decided to hire coaches for the summer season (Easter to October) from Hughes, dealers. The first batches were new Bedford SB5s with Duple C41F bodies (846/847HUA) and 856 to 859HUB with Plaxton C41F bodies.

For the 1965 season came AUM413 to 414C and Leyland PSU3/3R with Plaxton C51F bodies, and for the last year, 1967, came JUB301 to 304E and Bedford VAM14 with Plaxton C45F bodies.

The usage for this hired coach fleet per year was as follows:

- 1964 – 846/7HUA, 856 to 859HUB; at the end of the season, 857/859 were returned to Hughes.
- 1965 – 846/7HUA, 856/8HUB, AUM413 to 414C.
- 1966 – 846/7HUA, 856/8HUB, AUM413 to 414C; at the end of the season 846/7HUA were returned to Hughes.
- 1967 – 856/8HUB, AUM413 to 414C, JUB301 to 304E; at the end of the season all were returned to Hughes.

On return to Hughes these coaches were sold on to other operators.

Bedford/Duple HUA successfully touting for excursion work at Otley, as the A-board is now marked 'FULL'. (TLP)

Bedford/Plaxton 856HUB.

AUM414C at Otley.

Chapter 6

End Times for Ledgard

Otley was always the spiritual home of Ledgard for me and whilst there was only just over 20 per cent of the fleet based there, the fleet presence had a friendly invasive occupation. This was not just in the bus station with buses waiting on-stand, but with the double-parking opposite the bus station stands, and also across Crossgate on the spare ground by the post office on Nelson Street. This, coupled with the depot also being plainly visible just beyond the bus station, meant that Sammy Ledgard always had a delightfully large presence in Otley.

Strangely enough, the bus station centrepiece was a joint venture 53/47 per cent between the future nemesis West Yorkshire Road Car Co and Ledgard. On opening, Ledgard had the top four stands with stand one for the Moorfield Horsforth route worked by the Yeadon depot, stand two and three for the joint with West Yorkshire routes to Leeds and Ilkley and stand four for the former B & B Bradford to Harrogate route. West Yorkshire had the lower half stands from where it operated two routes to Bradford (via Yeadon and via Shipley), to Skipton (via Ilkley), to Harrogate (via the main road from Bradford and another route from Skipton/Ilkley, plus a country route via Blubberhouses).

To illustrate how busy Otley was, using Ledgard and West Yorkshire timetables from the late 1950s, on a Saturday the average departures per hour were around one bus every three minutes. When also taking into account the same rate of arrivals, this confirms that Otley was a very busy place and, therefore, a great place to 'watch the buses go by'.

However, sadly, this did not last forever, as in October 1967, Ledgard was swept away virtually overnight when it was sold to West Yorkshire. Some will say this was indecently done, but one thing is very sure: it was all done with a high degree of planning. On 14 October, Ledgard was still present, but by the very next day, they had largely vanished from the area, apart from 12 buses and two coaches which were kept for around two years by West Yorkshire, but this is another story.

References

Banks, John, Lockyer, Mike, *Samuel Ledgard, a Reminiscence* (2004)

Bate, Don, *Samuel Ledgard – Beer and Blue Buses* (2005, this is the definitive work)

Blacker, Ken, *London's Utility Buses* (1997)

Brindley, Roland, *Memories of Moorfield Bus Company*

Jenkinson, Keith, *Ledgard Way, The History of Samuel Ledgard* (1981)

John Kinsley's paintings: www.transport-art-collections.co.uk

Lockyer, M H, *The Ledgard Fleet* (1962)

Youhill, Chris, *Those very special Park Royal HGFs*

Old Buses website: http://www.old-bus-photos.co.uk/wp-content/themes/Old-Bus-Photos/articles_main_page.php

PSV Circle reference 2PB8, *Fleet History of Samuel Ledgard* (1992)

Ian Smith's website: http://www.countrybus.org/D/D.html#index

The Samuel Ledgard Society: http://www.samuelledgardsociety.org.uk